Cheese

Surprisingly Delicious Ways To Cook With Cheese

Copyright © 2020

All rights reserved.

DEDICATION

The author and publisher have provided this e-book to you for your personal use only. You may not make this e-book publicly available in any way. Copyright infringement is against the law. If you believe the copy of this e-book you are reading infringes on the author's copyright, please notify the publisher at: https://us.macmillan.com/piracy

Contents

Baked Ziti 4

Gnocchi with Gorgonzola Cream Sauce 7

Baked Brie 11

Skillet Scalloped Potatoes 12

Strawberry Shortcake Cake 14

Onion Soup with Beer 18

Mushroom Lovers' French Bread Pizza 20

Green Chile Queso...22

Cheesy Potato Gratin 24

Jalapeño Poppers 26

Creamy Stove-Top Mac and Cheese.............................28

Quesadillas With Shrimp and Peppers 30

Hamburger with Double Cheddar Cheese 32

Cheese

Pizza Soup 35

Deep-Fried Mozzarella Sticks 37

Hot Corn Chile Dip 39

Giada's Chicken Parmesan 41

Poutine Baked Potatoes 44

Blackberry Cheesecake Squares 47

Loaded Nacho Grilled Cheese 50

Cowboy Nachos 53

Goat Cheese Enchiladas 58

Mac n' Cheese 62

Roasted Pears with Blue Cheese 65

Poutine Monkey Bread 68

Cherry-Pistachio Brie en Croute 70

Spanish Mac & Cheese with Chorizo

INGREDIENTS

5 cups elbow macaroni

2 tsp olive oil

2 large chorizo sausages, casings removed, crumbled

½ large onion, peeled and cut in half lengthwise

1 bay leaf

2 cloves garlic

2 cups milk

3 Tbsp unsalted butter

3 Tbsp all-purpose flour

Salt and black pepper, to taste

2 ½ cups grated aged Cheddar cheese

1 tsp sweet smoked paprika

2 Tbsp Dijon mustard

For the topping

2 Tbsp olive oil

1 cup panko breadcrumbs

¼ cup grated Parmesan cheese

2 Tbsp chopped parsley

1 tsp sweet smoked paprika

DIRECTIONS

1. Heat your oven to 350°F (180°C). Lightly butter a 2-quart (2 L) baking dish.

2. Cook the macaroni in boiling salted water until tender. Drain and rinse.

3. In a large saucepan, heat the oil over medium heat. Add the sausages and cook until lightly browned, about 5 minutes. Transfer to

a plate and set aside.

4. To make the sauce, make a cut in half the onion about 1 inch (2.5 cm) deep, and slide a bay leaf into the slit. Stick the garlic cloves into the onion.

5. In a large saucepan, combine the milk and onion, heat over medium heat. Meanwhile, in a second saucepan, melt the butter over low heat. Add the flour and cook the roux, stirring, for 3 minutes. Do not let it colour. Remove from heat. Pour some hot milk into the roux, stirring until the milk is thoroughly blended in. Stir the mixture into the remaining milk and simmer, stirring frequently for 15 minutes. Season with salt and pepper.

6. Remove the onions. Add the cheese, paprika and the mustard. Continue cooking over low heat, stirring until the cheese is melted. Add the macaroni and sausage; stir together well. Season well with salt and pepper. Transfer to the prepared baking dish.

For the topping

1. To make the topping, combine bread crumbs, Parmesan, parsley, and paprika. Sprinkle over the casserole and drizzle with olive oil. Bake until browned and bubbly, 25 to 30 minutes.

2. Remove from oven and serve immediately.

Baked Ziti

INGREDIENTS

2 Tbsp olive oil

3 cloves garlic, minced

1 large onion, diced

1 lb(s) ground beef

1 lb(s) Italian sausage

2 (14.5-oz) cans tomato sauce or marinara sauce

1 (28-oz) can whole tomatoes with juice

2 tsp Italian seasoning

½ tsp red pepper flakes

Salt and freshly ground black pepper

1 lb(s) ziti

1 ½ lb(s) mozzarella, grated

1 (15-oz) tub whole-milk ricotta

½ cup grated Parmesan

2 Tbsp chopped fresh parsley, plus more for sprinkling

2 eggs

DIRECTIONS

1. Heat the olive oil in a pot over medium heat. Add the garlic and onions and saute until starting to soften, 3 to 4 minutes. Add the ground beef and sausage and cook until browned. Drain off almost all of the fat, leaving a bit behind for flavor and moisture. Add the tomato sauce, tomatoes, Italian seasoning, red pepper flakes and some salt and pepper. Stir, bring to a simmer and simmer for 25 to 30 minutes. Remove 3 to 4 cups of the cooked sauce to a bowl to cool down.

2. Bring a large pot of water to a boil and add some salt. Cook the ziti until not quite al dente.

3. Preheat the oven to 375°F.

4. In a bowl, mix 2 cups of the grated mozzarella, the ricotta, Parmesan, parsley, eggs and some salt and pepper. Stir together just a couple of times (do not mix completely).

5. Drain the pasta and rinse under cool water to stop the cooking and cool it down. Pour it into the bowl with the cheese mixture and toss to slightly combine (there should still be large lumps). Add the cooled reserved meat sauce and toss to combine.

6. Add half the coated pasta to a large casserole dish or lasagna dish. Spoon half of the remaining sauce over the top, then top with half the remaining mozzarella. Repeat with another layer of the coated pasta and the remaining sauce and mozzarella.

7. Bake until bubbling, about 20 minutes. Let stand 5 minutes before sprinkling with chopped parsley to serve.

Gnocchi with Gorgonzola Cream Sauce

INGREDIENTS

Dough

4 lb(s) Yukon Gold potatoes, peeled and cut into 1-inch cubes

2 cups semolina flour

3 cups all-purpose flour

Kosher salt

Gorgonzola Cream Sauce

1 medium onion, finely chopped

1 tsp garlic, chopped

½ cup Gorgonzola cheese, crumbled

1 ½ cups chicken stock or water

3 cups heavy cream

4 Tbsp parsley, chopped

Kosher salt

Black pepper

Extra virgin olive oil

DIRECTIONS

Dough

1. Place potatoes in a large pot and cover with cold salted water.

2. Bring to a boil, lower heat to a simmer, and cook for about 15 minutes, until potatoes are cooked but still firm,

3. Drain potatoes and transfer to a baking sheet to cool.

4. Once cooled, pass potatoes through a food mill or ricer into a large bowl.

5. In a second bowl, stir together the semolina flour and 2 cups of the all-purpose flour; reserve additional 1 cup of all-purpose flour for

dusting.

6. Pour the semolina mixture into the bowl with the potatoes and stir until fully combined.

7. Transfer dough to a cutting board and form into a large 3-inch thick loaf; let dough rest for 10 minutes.

8. To cook the gnocchi, bring a large pot of salted water to boil.

9. Slice loaf into 1-inch slices.

10. Dust a cutting board with the reserved all-purpose flour and roll dough into ½-inch thick logs.

11. Cutting on a bias, slice the log into ½-inch pieces and transfer gnocchi onto a well-floured baking sheet.

12. Repeat with remaining dough.

13. Working in batches, drop gnocchi into the boiling water to cook for 3 minutes, or until gnocchi floats to the top.

14. Using a slotted spoon, transfer gnocchi to an oiled baking sheet to cool; repeat process with remaining dough.

Gorgonzola Cream Sauce

1. To make sauce, stir and cook onions and garlic with 2 to 3 tablespoons of oil over medium heat until onions soften.

2. Add Gorgonzola cheese and continue cooking while stirring until cheese is starts to melt.

3. Stir in chicken stock and cream.

4. Bring mixture to a boil and simmer for 5 minutes, until cheese is melted and sauce begins to thicken.

5. Add cooled gnocchi to the sauce and continue to simmer until gnocchi are hot and sauce has thickened enough to coat the dumplings.

6. Add salt and pepper, to taste.

7. Garnish with parsley and serve.

Baked Brie

INGREDIENTS

¼ wheel brie

4 Tbsp honey

DIRECTIONS

1. Preheat the oven to 350°F.

2. Place the brie on a sheet pan covered with parchment paper and drizzle with the honey. Bake for 5 to 7 minutes, or until it starts to ooze but not melt.

3. Serve with crackers.

Skillet Scalloped Potatoes

INGREDIENTS

6 medium Yukon Gold potatoes, peeled and thinly sliced

4 Tbsp unsalted butter

3 Tbsp all-purpose flour

2 ½ cup milk

2 cup Gruyere cheese, shredded

salt and pepper

DIRECTIONS

1. Preheat oven to 400°F.

2. Heat an 8 to 9-inch oven safe skillet over medium heat. Add 3 tablespoons of butter and reduce heat to low; cook until melted and frothy. Add flour and whisk until lightly browned and raw taste is cooked about, about 30 seconds. Season with salt and pepper. Whisk in milk until smooth.

3. Remove skillet from heat and pour milk mixture into a bowl or large measuring cup.

4. In a separate bowl, toss sliced potatoes with salt and pepper. Arrange potato slices in the skillet so that they slightly overlap. Using 1 ½ cups of the cheese, sprinkle between every second layer of potato. Pour milk mixture back into the skillet to coat potatoes. Top potatoes with remaining ½ cup cheese. Dot the cheese with the remaining tablespoon of butter; season with pepper.

5. Cover with boil and bake for 60 minutes. Remove foil and bake or broil for 5-10 minutes until top is golden and bubbly. Remove from the oven and let stand for 10 minutes before serving.

Strawberry Shortcake Cake

INGREDIENTS

Strawberry Shortcake

9 Tbsp unsalted butter, softened, plus more for greasing

1 ½ cups all-purpose flour, plus more for dusting

3 Tbsp cornstarch

1 tsp baking soda

½ tsp salt

1 ½ cups + 2 Tbsp granulated sugar

3 whole large eggs

½ cup sour cream, at room temperature

1 tsp vanilla extract

1 lb(s) strawberries, plus more to garnish, optional

Icing

1 ½ lb(s) powdered sugar, sifted

8 oz cream cheese, at room temperature

2 sticks unsalted butter, softened

1 tsp vanilla extract

Dash salt

DIRECTIONS

Strawberry Shortcake

1. Preheat the oven to 350°F. Grease and flour an 8-inch cake pan.

2. Sift together the flour, cornstarch, baking soda and salt. In a stand mixer fitted with a paddle attachment, cream the butter with 1 1/2 cups of the granulated sugar until light and fluffy. Add the eggs one at a time, mixing well after each addition. Add the sour cream and vanilla, and mix until combined. Add the sifted dry ingredients and mix on low speed until just barely combined.

3. Pour the batter into the prepared cake pan. Bake until no longer jiggly like my bottom, 45 to 50 minutes. Remove the cake from the pan as soon as you pull it out of the oven. Place the cake on a cooling rack and allow it to cool completely.

4. Stem and halve the strawberries, and mash then them. Sprinkle the strawberries with the remaining 2 tablespoons granulated sugar and allow to sit for 30 minutes.

Icing

1. Combine the powdered sugar, cream cheese, butter, vanilla and dash of salt in a mixing bowl. Mix until very light and fluffy.

2. Slice the cake in half to make 2 smaller cakes. Spread the strawberries evenly over each cut side of the cake halves, pouring on all the juices as well. Place the cake halves into the freezer for 5 minutes, just to make icing the cake easier.

3. Remove the cake halves from the freezer. Use a little less than one-third of the icing to spread over the top of the strawberries on the bottom layer. Place the second layer of cake on top. Add half of the remaining icing to the top spreading evenly, then spread the remaining icing around the sides.

4. Leave plain or garnish with strawberry halves. Serve slightly cool.

TIPS AND SUBSTITUTIONS

- Special equipment: 8-inch cake pan that's at least 2-inches deep! Before baking, the batter should not fill the pan more than halfway.
- This cake is best when served slightly cool. The butter content in the icing will cause it to soften at room temperature. For best results, store in the fridge!
- This recipe has been updated and may differ from what was originally published or broadcast.

Onion Soup with Beer

INGREDIENTS

10 cup onions, sliced (about 10 medium onions)

¼ cup butter

1 Tbsp flour

1 bottle pale ale

1 Tbsp Dijon mustard

4 cup chicken broth, approximately

6 thick diagonal slices baguette, toasted

2 cup grated sharp cheddar

1 pinch Salt and pepper

DIRECTIONS

1. In a large non-stick saucepan, brown the onions in the butter until golden and soft, about 30 minutes. Season with salt and pepper. Dust with the flour and cook for 1 more minute. Add the beer and bring to a boil, stirring constantly. Add the broth and bring to a boil. Reduce the heat and simmer for about 10 minutes. Add more broth if necessary. Adjust the seasoning.

2. With the rack in the middle position, preheat the broiler.

3. Ladle the soup into 4 ovenproof bowls. Place 1 toast in each bowl and top with cheese. Place the bowls on a baking sheet. Broil until the cheese is golden brown.

Mushroom Lovers' French Bread Pizza

INGREDIENTS

8 portobello mushroom caps

1 lb(s) button mushrooms

½ lb(s) shiitake mushrooms

3 Tbsp extra-virgin olive oil, 3 turns of the pan

2 Tbsp butter, cut into pieces

1 leaf bay

4 cloves garlic, finely chopped

Salt and pepper

½ cup dry white wine, eyeball it

2 tsp Worcestershire sauce, eyeball it

1 Tbsp chopped fresh thyme leaves, 4 sprigs stripped and chopped

1 loaf crusty French bread, 24 inches

3 cups shredded Gruyere or Swiss chard

DIRECTIONS

1. Wipe mushrooms clean with a damp towel. Slice the mushrooms. Heat a deep skillet with extra-virgin olive oil and butter over medium heat. When butter melts into oil, add bay, garlic and mushrooms. Cook until mushrooms are dark and tender, 12 to 15 minutes. Season the mushrooms with salt and pepper and add wine. Deglaze the pan with wine, eyeball the amount. Shake the pan and add the Worcestershire and thyme. Turn off heat.

2. Preheat broiler and split the loaf lengthwise and across. Hollow out a bit of the soft insides. Toast the bread lightly under broiler. Fill bread with mushrooms evenly then top with cheese liberally. Melt cheese until it browns and bubbles then remove the pizzas from the oven and turn off the broiler.

Green Chile Queso

INGREDIENTS

2 Tbsp butter

2 onions, diced

2 (15-oz) cans diced green chiles

2 - 4 chipotle peppers in adobo, finely chopped

4 lb(s) processed cheese, such as Velveeta, cut into chunks

2 cans green chile enchilada sauce

DIRECTIONS

1. Set a large skillet over medium heat and add the butter. Once

melted, add the onions and cook until starting to soften, 2 to 3 minutes. Add the green chiles and chipotle peppers and cook for a minute. Add the cheese and let it melt. Add the enchilada sauce and give it all a stir. Transfer to a slow cooker to keep warm.

Cheesy Potato Gratin

INGREDIENTS

6 Tbsp unsalted butter

⅓ cup all-purpose flour

1 qt milk

3 cups shredded sharp Cheddar cheese

3 cups shredded Gruyere cheese

2 cloves garlic, smashed

½ tsp freshly ground pepper

Kosher salt

½ tsp freshly grated nutmeg

7 medium Yukon Gold potatoes, unpeeled, cut in 1/2-inch thick coins

¼ cup chopped fresh parsley, for garnish

DIRECTIONS

1. Preheat the oven to 300°F.

2. Melt 4 tablespoons of the butter in a large, oven-safe high-sided skillet over medium-high heat. When the foam subsides, add the flour and cook, stirring constantly, until it has the consistency of wet sand, about 3 minutes. Remove from the heat and whisk in the milk, little by little.

3. Put the saucepan over high heat and bring to a boil, whisking constantly. Lower the heat and whisk in 2 cups of the Cheddar, 2 cups of the Gruyere, the garlic, pepper and salt. Whisk until the cheese is melted, then stir in the nutmeg. Add the sliced potatoes to the pan. Scatter the remaining 2 tablespoons butter and the remaining 1 cup Cheddar and 1 cup Gruyere over the top.

4. Bake in the oven for 45 minutes, then increase the oven temperature to 400°F., and bake until the potatoes are fork-tender and the top is bubbly and golden brown, about 15 minutes more. (Cover the dish with foil if the top becomes too dark before the potatoes are tender.) Scatter the chopped parsley over the top, and

serve.

Jalapeño Poppers

INGREDIENTS

20 fresh jalapenos, 2 to 3 inches in size

2 8-oz packages cream cheese, slightly softened

1 lb(s) thin (regular) bacon, slices cut in half

DIRECTIONS

1. Preheat the oven to 275°F. Set a wire rack over a baking sheet.

2. If you have them, slip on some latex gloves for the pepper prep. Cut the jalapenos in half lengthwise. With a spoon, remove the seeds and white membranes (the source of the heat; leave a little if you like things HOT). Smear cream cheese into each jalapeno half and then wrap with a bacon piece (1/2 slice). Secure by sticking a toothpick through the middle. Place on the rack in the baking sheet.

3. Bake until the bacon is sizzling and done, 1 hour 15 minutes. Serve immediately, or they're also great at room temperature.

Creamy Stove-Top Mac and Cheese

INGREDIENTS

Kosher salt

1 lb(s) medium shell pasta

4 Tbsp butter

¼ cup all-purpose flour

1 ½ cups whole milk

1 cup half-and-half

2 cups cheddar cheese, grated (about 8 ounces)

1 cup colby jack cheese, grated (about 4 ounces)

1 tsp dijon mustard, heaping

⅛ tsp paprika

1 dash hot sauce

4 oz cream cheese, cut into cubes

Freshly ground black pepper

DIRECTIONS

1. Bring a large pot of salted water to a boil. Add the pasta and cook until al dente. Drain and reserve.

2. Melt the butter in a large saucepan over medium-high heat. When it begins to foam, sprinkle in the flour and stir until it becomes pasty, about 1 minute. Whisk in the milk and half-and-half and bring to a low simmer. Stir until the mixture looks thick, about 5 minutes. Add the Cheddar and Colby Jack cheese by handfuls, stirring well after each addition until melted. Mix in the mustard, paprika and hot sauce. Then fold in the cream cheese and stir well until melted. Season with salt and pepper. Lastly stir in the cooked pasta.

3. Serve the mac and cheese immediately while still warm and at its creamiest.

Quesadillas With Shrimp and Peppers

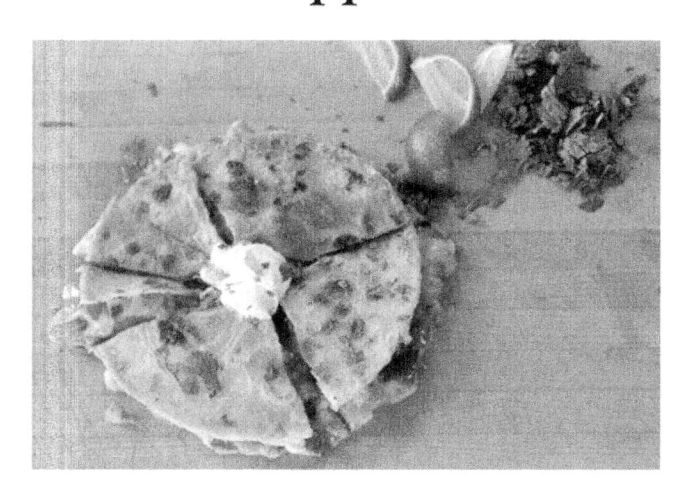

INGREDIENTS

1 cup Mexican red sauce

12 large shrimp, peeled and deveined

2 Tbsp olive oil

1 large onion, chopped into chunks

1 green bell pepper, chopped into chunks

1 red bell pepper, chopped into chunks

Butter, for cooking tortillas

6 flour tortillas

2 cups grated cheese, (Monterey Jack is best)

Sour cream, for serving

Fresh cilantro, for serving

Lime wedges, for serving

DIRECTIONS

1. On a large plate, pour the red sauce over the shrimp and set aside.

2. Heat a skillet over high heat and add the olive oil. Cook the onions and bell peppers over high heat until they start to get nicely browned. Remove from the skillet and set aside.

3. Add the shrimp with the sauce. Cook, stirring only occasionally, until the shrimp are opaque. Add in a little water if the sauce gets dry. Remove from the skillet and chop the shrimp into bite-size pieces.

4. In a clean skillet, heat some butter. Place a tortilla in the skillet, then layer on the ingredients: cheese, vegetables and shrimp. Top with a little more cheese and a second tortilla. Cook on both sides, adding butter before flipping to the other side so the tortilla isn't overly dry. Remove from the skillet and slice into wedges. Repeat with the rest of the tortillas and filling ingredients.

5. Serve with sour cream, cilantro and lime wedges.

Hamburger with Double Cheddar Cheese

INGREDIENTS

Ingredients and Directions

2 lb(s) freshly ground chuck

Salt and freshly ground black pepper

8 slices white Cheddar, sliced 1/4-inch thick

8 slices yellow Cheddar, sliced 1/4-inch thick

8 hamburger buns

Horseradish Mustard (recipe follows)

8 leaves Romaine lettuce

Grilled Vidalia Onions (recipe follows)

Dill pickles, sliced

Ketchup

Horseradish Mustard

½ cup Dijon mustard

2 Tbsp prepared horseradish, drained

Grilled Vidalia Onions

2 Vidalia onions, sliced crosswise, 1/4-inch thick slices

2 Tbsp olive oil

Salt and freshly ground black pepper

DIRECTIONS

Ingredients and Directions

1. Preheat grill or a cast iron skillet to high.

2. Divide the beef into 8 (4-ounce) burgers. Season on both sides

with salt and pepper, to taste. Grill or cook in the skillet for 3 to 4 minutes on each side for medium-rare doneness. During last minutes of cooking add 2 slices of cheese to each burger, cover grill and let melt, approximately 1 minute. Place burger on bun and top with Horseradish Mustard, lettuce, Grilled Vidalia Onions, pickles and ketchup.

Horseradish Mustard

1. Whisk mustard and horseradish together in a small bowl.

Grilled Vidalia Onions

1. Brush olive oil on both sides of the onions and season with salt and pepper. Grill the onion slices for 3 to 4 minutes on each side until golden brown.

Pizza Soup

INGREDIENTS

2 Tbsp (30 mL) olive oil

2 onions, chopped

6 - 8 cloves garlic, minced

1 (28-oz/796 mL) can crushed tomatoes

1 Tbsp (15 mL) dried oregano

3 cups (750 mL) or so your favourite pizza toppings (such as sliced bell peppers, mushrooms, olives, cooked bacon)

4 oz (115 g) spicy pepperoni, thinly sliced into rounds and halved

4 cups (1 L) rich chicken broth or plain old water

lots of freshly ground pepper

DIRECTIONS

1. Preheat your broiler.

2. Splash the olive oil into your soup pot over medium-high heat. Add the onions and garlic. Cook, stirring, as the onions soften, 2 or 3 minutes. Pour in the tomatoes, then stir in the oregano, your pizza toppings and the pepperoni.

3. Pour in the chicken broth and season with salt and pepper. Bring to a vigorous boil for a moment, then immediately reduce the heat to a slow, steady simmer and cover. Cook, stirring occasionally, until the flavours brighten and the textures soften, 10 minutes or so.

Deep-Fried Mozzarella Sticks

INGREDIENTS

1 lb(s) Mozzarella cheese, cut into sticks, 1/2" thick

1 cup flour

3 eggs, whisked

1 cup breadcrumbs

1 heaping spoonful of dried oregano

DIRECTIONS

1. Preheat your deep fryer to 375 degrees.

2. Set up a standard breading station by pouring the flour into one bowl, the eggs into a second and the breadcrumbs and oregano into a third.

3. To keep your hands from becoming breaded use one to handle the sticks while they are dry and the other hand while they are wet. Dredge the mozzarella sticks in the flour first then shake off any excess before adding to the egg. Coat well with the egg, drain well then toss into the breadcrumbs. Coat well then let rest. It is best to bread all the sticks once than go back and bread them all again and then a third time. A few minutes rest in between coats will help the bread crumbs adhere.

4. Fry until golden brown and crispy.

Hot Corn Chile Dip

INGREDIENTS

5 ears fresh corn, shucked

4 Tbsp butter

2 cloves garlic, minced

2 jalapenos, seeded and diced finely

1 medium onion, diced

1 green bell pepper, seeded and diced

1 red bell pepper, seeded and diced

2 cans diced green chiles

1 ½ cups pepper-jack cheese, grated -

4 oz cream cheese, softened

½ cup mayonnaise

½ cup sour cream

3 green onions, sliced thin

Tortilla chips or pita crisps, for serving

DIRECTIONS

1. Heat a grill on medium heat. Grill the corn until lots of the kernels have color. Cut off the kernels and set aside.

2. If serving immediately, preheat the oven to 350° F.

3. Melt the butter in a large skillet over medium-high heat. Add the garlic, jalapenos, onions and green and red bell peppers. Cook for a few minutes, until the peppers get great color on the outside. Add the chiles and stir for 30 seconds. Set aside.

4. In a large bowl, combine 1 cup of the pepper-jack, the cream cheese, mayonnaise, sour cream and green onions and stir until combined. Add the corn mixture and stir to combine thoroughly. Pour into a small baking dish. Bake immediately, or cover with foil and refrigerate up to 48 hours.

5. Sprinkle the remaining 1/2 cup cheese over the top and bake until bubbly, 20 to 25 minutes. Serve with tortilla chips or pita crisps.

Giada's Chicken Parmesan

INGREDIENTS

Chicken

3 Tbsp olive oil

1 tsp fresh rosemary leaves, chopped

1 tsp fresh thyme leaves, chopped

1 tsp fresh Italian parsley leaves, chopped

Salt and freshly ground black pepper

8 (3-oz) chicken cutlets

1 ½ cups Simple Tomato Sauce (recipe follows) or purchased marinara sauce

½ cup mozzarella, shredded

16 tsp Parmesan, grated

2 Tbsp unsalted butter, cut into pieces

Simple Tomato Sauce

½ cup extra-virgin olive oil

1 small onion, chopped

2 cloves garlic, chopped

1 stalk celery, chopped

1 carrot, chopped

Sea salt and freshly ground black pepper

2 (32-oz) cans crushed tomatoes

4 - 6 fresh basil leaves

2 dried bay leaves

4 Tbsp unsalted butter (optional)

DIRECTIONS

Chicken

1. Preheat the oven to 500°F.

2. Stir the oil and herbs in a small bowl to blend. Season with salt and pepper. Brush both sides of the cutlets with the herb oil. Heat a large heavy oven-proof skillet over high heat. Add the cutlets and cook just until brown, about 2 minutes per side. Remove the skillet from the heat.

3. Spoon the marinara sauce over and around the cutlets. Sprinkle 1 teaspoon of the mozzarella over each cutlet, then sprinkle 2 teaspoons of the Parmesan over each. Sprinkle the butter pieces atop the cutlets. Bake until the cheese melts and the chicken is cooked through, about 3 to 5 minutes.

Simple Tomato Sauce

1. In a large casserole pot, heat the oil over medium high heat. Add the onion and garlic and saute until soft and translucent, about 2 minutes. Add the celery and carrots and season with salt and pepper. Saute until all the vegetables are soft, about 5 minutes. Add the tomatoes, basil, and bay leaves and simmer covered on low heat for 1 hour or until thick. Remove the bay leaves and check for seasoning. If the sauce still tastes acidic, add unsalted butter, 1 tablespoon at a

time to round out the flavors.

2. Add half the tomato sauce into the bowl of a food processor. Process until smooth. Continue with the remaining tomato sauce.

3. If not using all the sauce, allow it to cool completely and pour 1 to 2 cup portions into freezer plastic bags. This will freeze up to 6 months.

Poutine Baked Potatoes

INGREDIENTS

Baked Potatoes

4 large Idaho (baker) potatoes, washed

2 Tbsp butter, room temperature

coarse salt

Poutine Gravy

2 Tbsp butter

2 Tbsp all-purpose flour

1 ½ cup good quality low-sodium beef broth

1 tsp chopped fresh thyme

salt & pepper

Assembly

2 Tbsp butter

8 oz fresh cheese curd (orange, white or a mix)

DIRECTIONS

Baked Potatoes

1. Preheat oven to 350 °F.

2. Pierce potatoes with a fork, then rub with butter and sprinkle with salt. Place each potato into an individual baking dish and bake for about an hour, until they yield when gently pressed. While baking, prepare gravy.

Poutine Gravy

1. To make the gravy, add butter and flour to a small saucepot over medium heat. Stir constantly with a wooden spoon until a rich brown, the color of peanut butter (this takes 7 to 10 minutes).

2. Slowly pour in stock in a thin stream, whisking constantly, then stir in thyme. Bring to a simmer, season to taste and keep warm.

Assembly

1. To assemble, cut an oval opening into top of each potato (you can reserve these for another use, such as Smoked Salmon Potato Skins). Scoop out most of the potato and mash with butter, and season lightly.

2. Spoon mashed potato back into their skins. Ladle gravy into each potato and top with cheese curd.

3. Return potato to oven to melt cheese, about 10 minutes, then serve immediately.

Blackberry Cheesecake Squares

INGREDIENTS

Crust

Cooking spray, for spraying foil

1 box vanilla wafers (11 oz.)

½ cup pecans

1 stick butter, melted (1/2 cup)

Filling

3 packages cream cheese (8 oz. each)

1 ½ cups sugar

1 ½ tsp vanilla

4 eggs

½ cup sour cream

Topping

4 cups blackberries

1 cup sugar

1 Tbsp cornstarch

DIRECTIONS

Crust

1. Preheat the oven to 350°F.

2. Line a 9-by-13-inch rectangular baking pan with foil and spray with cooking spray.

3. Place the vanilla wafers and pecans into the bowl of a food processor and pulse until the mixture becomes crumbs. Add the melted butter and vanilla and pulse again until combined. Pour the mixture into the prepared pan and press the crumbs into the bottom of the pan. (If they come up the sides, that's okay!)

Filling

1. Beat the cream cheese and sugar together in a medium bowl with an electric mixer until smooth. Add the eggs one at a time, beating after each addition. Add the sour cream and mix again.

2. Pour the filling into the crust, smooth the top and bake for 50 minutes. Turn off the oven, open the oven door and allow the pan to sit in the open oven for 15 minutes. Remove and set aside to cool.

Topping

1. Add the blackberries, sugar and 1/4 cup water to a saucepan or skillet. Bring to a boil over medium-high heat and cook until the juices thicken slightly, 4 to 5 minutes.

2. In a small bowl, make a slurry by stirring together the cornstarch and 2 tablespoons water until smooth. Add the slurry to the berries, return to the boil and cook for another 1 to 2 minutes. Turn off the heat and cool the mixture.

3. Pour the blackberries over the cheesecake and place the pan into the fridge to cool and set for at least 2 hours (several hours is better).

4. When ready to serve, remove the cheesecake from the pan by lifting the edges of the foil. Slice into 15 pieces with a long serrated knife.

Loaded Nacho Grilled Cheese

INGREDIENTS

2 slices French bread

1 Tbsp sour cream

2 Tbsp salsa

Tex Mex cheese

2 - 3 Tbsp cooked ground beef

⅛ tsp taco seasoning

1 stalk green onion, chopped

4 - 5 cilantro leaves

1 slice tomato, diced

¼ avocado, diced

1 - 2 black olives, chopped

1 Tbsp black beans

1 - 2 slices jalapeno pepper, chopped

1 - 2 handfuls nacho-flavoured Doritos, crumbled

1 egg, scrambled

butter

DIRECTIONS

1. If you don't have any ground beef, cook that to your liking first (I just used salt, pepper and garlic). Now let's start with the sandwich: crush all the Doritos and spread them on a plate, dip one side of each bread slice in the egg and then into the Doritos. Once you've done

this, begin assembling the sandwich with sour cream on one slice and salsa on the other. Next place a layer of cheese on the bottom slice, then stack on the rest of ingredients and finish with another layer of cheese and your top slice.

2. In a pan on medium heat, add some butter. Once that has melted, place your sandwich in, cooking each side until browned and the cheese is melting. You may want to cover your pan with a lid while it's cooking to help the cheese melt, since there is so much stuff in the sandwich.

3. Once everything is ooey gooey, slice it in half and enjoy all your favourite nacho toppings in one glorious sandwich. If you're feeling ambitious, you can even make your own salsa and guacamole for dipping!

Cowboy Nachos

INGREDIENTS

2 cups Pinto Beans, recipe follows

freshly ground black pepper, to taste

Tabasco sauce, to taste

minced garlic, to taste

jarred or fresh jalapenos (chopped or sliced), to taste, optional

canola oil, for warming brisket

2 cups shredded Braised Beef Brisket (plus pan drippings as needed), recipe follows

Cheese

1 can Mexican red sauce or enchilada sauce (enough to moisten brisket)

½ bag tortilla chips, as needed

2 cups Monterey Jack cheese, grated (however much you want)

2 cups Pico de Gallo, recipe follows

Pinto Beans

4 cups pinto beans, dried

4 slices bacon, thick (you can also use salt pork, ham hock)

Salt and freshly ground black pepper

Braised Beef Brisket

2 cans beef consomme

1 ½ cups soy sauce

½ cup fresh lemon juice

2 Tbsp liquid smoke

5 cloves garlic, chopped

10 pounds beef brisket

Pico de Gallo

5 plum tomatoes (Roma)

3 jalapeno peppers

½ large onion or 1 small onion

1 bunch cilantro, fresh

½ lime

Salt

DIRECTIONS

1. Heat up the Pinto Beans and doctor them to your desired "temperature," adding some ground black pepper, Tabasco sauce, minced garlic and jalapenos if using. Make them as spicy or mild as you like.

2. Preheat the broiler.

3. In a very hot skillet, add a bit of canola oil and the Braised Beef Brisket. Cook for 1 to 2 minutes, and then flip and cook for another 1 to 2 minutes. Next, pour some of the red sauce over the meat to make it nice and moist. If you have them, also add a bit of the pan drippings from the brisket-cooking process (or a bit of beef broth — again just enough to bring the meat to a nice moist consistency). Stir to combine and remove from the heat.

4. To assemble: In a heatproof dish, layer half of the tortilla chips, beans, brisket, cheese and Pico de Gallo. Repeat the layers but leave off the second layer of Pico de Gallo until after the dish is cooked.

5. Place on the middle or bottom rack of your oven and broil until the cheese is melted. Watch closely so they don't burn. Sprinkle the remaining Pico de Gallo over the top before serving.

6. Inhale, exhale and then ravenously consume!

Pinto Beans

1. Rinse the beans in cool water; pour into a pot and cover with water by 2 to 3 inches. Cut the bacon into large pieces and add to the pot. Bring to a boil, then reduce the heat and cover. Simmer until the beans are tender, about 2 hours, adding water to the pot as needed. (The beans should have a thick broth.)

2. Toward the end of the cooking time, add 1 teaspoon salt and 2 teaspoons pepper. Check the seasoning before serving, and add more salt and pepper if desired. Don't over-salt. Yield: 12 servings.

Braised Beef Brisket

1. Combine the beef consomme, soy sauce, lemon juice, liquid smoke and garlic in a large roasting pan (a disposable is just fine). Place the brisket in the marinade, fat-side up. Cover tightly with foil. Marinate

in the refrigerator for 24 to 48 hours.

2. When ready to cook, preheat the oven to 300°F.

3. Cook the brisket in the foil-covered pan until fork-tender, about 40 minutes per pound (6 to 7 hours). Transfer to a cutting board, slice against the grain and put the slices back into the cooking liquid. Serve immediately, spooning the juice over the slices.

4. You may store the pan in the fridge for up to 2 days, or freeze for use at a later date. If fat collects and hardens at the top, remove and discard.

Pico de Gallo

1. Chop the tomatoes, jalapenos and onions into a very small dice. (Leave the seeds in your jalapenos for a hotter pico.) Adjust the amount of jalapenos to your preferred temperature.

2. Next, chop up a nice-sized bunch of cilantro. Just remove and discard the long leafless stems before chopping. No need to remove the leaves from the stems completely.

3. Put the tomatoes, jalapenos, onions and cilantro together in a bowl and give it a good stir. Squeeze the juice of the lime half into the bowl. Add salt to taste and stir again. Yield: 6 servings.

Goat Cheese Enchiladas

INGREDIENTS

Enchiladas

12 blue corn tortillas

Red Chile-Tomato Sauce, recipe follows

Goat Cheese Filling, recipe follows

8 oz Monterey Jack, grated

3 Tbsp chopped fresh cilantro leaves

Sour cream, for garnish

Chopped green onions, for garnish

Red Chile-Tomato Sauce

3 ancho chiles

3 Tbsp vegetable oil

1 large red onion, finely chopped

3 cloves garlic, finely chopped

1 Tbsp ground cumin

1 Tbsp dried Mexican oregano

1 cup dry white wine

2 (16-oz) cans plum tomatoes, pureed

3 cups homemade chicken or vegetable stock

1 - 2 Tbsp honey

Salt and freshly ground black pepper

Filling

1 ¼ lb(s) goat cheese

3 cloves garlic, coarsely chopped

¼ cup freshly grated cotija cheese

2 Tbsp fresh lime juice

Salt and freshly ground black pepper

¼ cup finely chopped cilantro leaves

DIRECTIONS

Enchiladas

1. Preheat oven to 375°F.

2. Dip tortillas in chile sauce to lightly coat both sides. Spoon about 2 tablespoons of the goat cheese filling on each tortilla and roll up. Spread 1/2 cup of the tomato-chile sauce into a medium, deep casserole dish. Arrange rolled tortillas in the casserole so they fit snugly. Repeat with remaining tortillas. Pour 1 1/2 cups of the sauce over the enchiladas and top with the grated cheese. Bake for 20 to 30 minutes or until the enchiladas are heated through. Remove from the oven and sprinkle with chopped cilantro. Garnish with sour cream and green onions.

Red Chile-Tomato Sauce

1. Bring 2 cups of water to a boil in a small saucepan. Add chiles, remove from heat and let sit for 30 minutes. Remove stems and seeds, then place in food processor with 1/4 cup of the soaking liquid and puree until smooth.

2. Heat oil in a medium saucepan over medium-high heat. Add onion

and cook until soft. Add garlic and cook for 1 minute. Add cumin and oregano and cook for 1 minute. Add ancho puree and cook for 2 to 3 minutes. Add wine, pureed tomatoes, and stock and cook for 25 to 30 minutes or until slightly thickened. Season with honey, salt, and pepper, to taste. For a chunkier sauce, leave as is. For a smoother sauce, puree with an immersion blender, or puree in batches in a blender or food processor. Keep warm until ready to serve.

Filling

1. Place goat cheese, garlic, cotija, and lime juice in a food processor and process until smooth. Season with salt and pepper and fold in the cilantro.

Mac n' Cheese

INGREDIENTS

2 ½ cups uncooked macaroni (6 cups cooked)

1 cup broccoli florets

10 strips uncooked bacon, chopped

4 cups milk

3 bay leaves

¼ cup melted butter

¼ cup flour

3 ½ cups grated Cheddar cheese

1 Tbsp lemon juice

1 Tbsp salt

1 tsp pepper

1 cup crushed mustard pretzels

Salt

DIRECTIONS

1. Preheat oven to 350°F.

2. To cook the noodles, bring a large pot of salted water to boil; add macaroni noodles and cook, stirring occasionally, until noodles are tender but still firm, about 6 minutes.

3. Drain pasta and set aside.

4. To cook the broccoli, bring a second pot of water to boil; add broccoli and cook until tender but still firm, about 4 minutes.

5. Drain broccoli and rinse under cold water immediately.

6. To cook the bacon, heat a large pan over medium heat; add strips of bacon and cook, stirring often, until bacon reaches desired crispness.

7. To make the sauce for the macaroni and cheese, add milk and bay leaves to a medium saucepan and heat over medium heat for 20 minutes, to flavour the milk.

8. While milk steeps, mix together melted butter and flour in a small bowl.

9. Once milk has steeped, slowly whisk flour mixture into the milk.

10. Simmer over medium low heat for 10 minutes, until sauce starts to thicken.

11. Stir in 2 ½ cups of the grated Cheddar cheese, lemon juice, salt, and pepper; mix well.

12. Once the cheese has melted completely, remove sauce from heat and pour through a fine mesh strainer into a large saucepan.

13. Stir in reserved cooked macaroni, bacon, and broccoli.

14. Bring the mixture to a simmer over medium heat for 2 minutes.

15. Pour the macaroni mixture into a greased casserole dish.

16. Sprinkle reserved 1 cup of Cheddar over top, followed by the crushed pretzels.

17. Bake for 10 to 15 minutes in the preheated oven, until the top is golden brown and the mixture is bubbling.

18. Remove from oven and serve.

Roasted Pears with Blue Cheese

INGREDIENTS

3 ripe but firm Anjou pears

Freshly squeezed lemon juice (3 lemons)

3 oz coarsely crumbled sharp blue cheese, such as Stilton

¼ cup dried cranberries

¼ cup walnut halves, toasted and chopped

½ cup apple cider

3 Tbsp port

⅓ cup light brown sugar, lightly packed

¼ cup good olive oil

6 oz baby arugula

Kosher salt

DIRECTIONS

1. Preheat the oven to 375°F.

2. Peel the pears and slice them lengthwise into halves. With a small sharp paring knife and a melon baller, remove the core and seeds from each pear, leaving a round well for the filling. Trim a small slice away from the rounded sides of each pear half so that they will sit in the baking dish without wobbling. Toss the pears with some lemon juice to prevent them from turning brown. Arrange them, core side up, in a baking dish large enough to hold the pears snugly.

3. Gently toss the crumbled blue cheese, dried cranberries, and walnuts together in a small bowl. Divide the mixture among the pears, mounding it on top of the indentation.

4. In the same small bowl, combine the apple cider, port, and brown sugar, stirring to dissolve the sugar. Pour the mixture over and around the pears. Bake the pears, basting occasionally with the cider mixture, for 30 minutes, or until tender. Set aside until warm or at room temperature.

5. Just before serving, whisk together the olive oil, 1/4 cup of lemon juice, and 1/4 cup of the basting liquid in a large bowl. Divide the arugula among 6 plates and top each with a pear half. Drizzle each pear with some of the basting liquid, sprinkle with salt, and serve warm.

Poutine Monkey Bread

INGREDIENTS

2 lb(s) refrigerated country-style biscuits

1 cup Cheddar cheese curds

3 ¼ cups chicken gravy

DIRECTIONS

1. Preheat oven to 375°F. Grease a 10-inch cast iron skillet.

2. Cut each biscuit into 4 equal wedges. Place in a large bowl with 2/3 cup of gravy (set aside remaining) and cheese curds. Toss until curds and dough are coated with gravy.

3. Pour mixture into prepared skillet, ensuring cheese curds are evenly distributed. Place skillet on a rimmed baking sheet and bake until the top is golden brown, about 20 minutes. Let cool for 5 minutes.

4. Reheat remaining gravy that was set aside and pour over monkey bread or use for dipping.

Cherry-Pistachio Brie en Croute

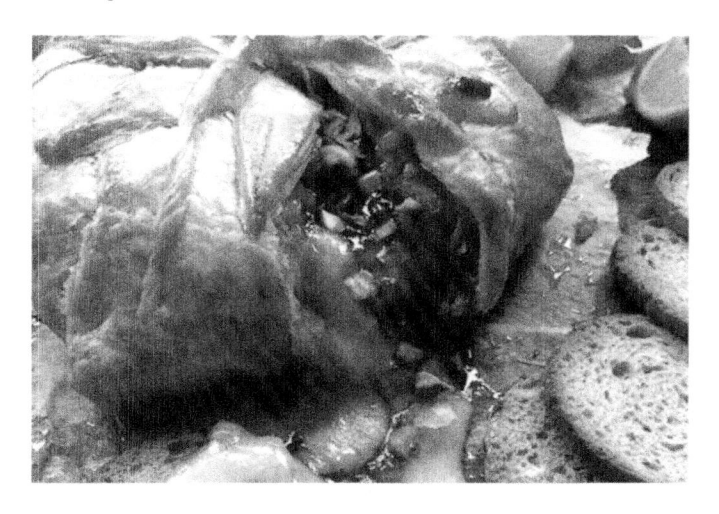

INGREDIENTS:

1 10-inch x 10-inch sheet puff pastry

1 200 g wheel double cream Brie

1/2 sour cherry preserves (or jam/jelly of your choice)

1/2 cup chopped pistachios (nut of your choice)

1 egg yolk

cherry-pistachio-brie-en-croute

DIRECTIONS

1. Line a baking sheet with parchment. Roll out puff pastry on a floured surface. Place Brie in centre of pastry. Place preserves on brie

and then place nuts over preserves. Bring the corners of the pastry into the centre of the Brie, then bring the side up to meet the corners. Trim excess pastry from the centre. Form decorative detailing with excess pastry to help seal the pastry. Chill in freezer for 30 minutes.

2. While chilling, preheat oven to 400°F.

3. Mix egg yolk with 1 Tbsp water and brush over pastry. Bake in centre of oven until pastry is golden, about 30 minutes.

4. Remove from oven and let cool for 10 minutes before serving. Do not bake in advance.

Printed in Great Britain
by Amazon